Arcola Theatre and Maya Ellis present

Stop and Search

Cast

Akim	**Munashe Chirisa**
Lee	**Tyler Luke Cunningham**
T	**David Kirkbride**
T	**Shaun Mason**
E	**Jessye Romeo**

T0262513

Writer	**Gabriel Gbadamosi**
Director	**Mehmet Ergen**
Designer	**Eleanor Bull**
Lighting Designer	**Richard Williamson**
Sound Designer	**Daniel Balfour**
Production Assistant	**Siar Kanik**
Assistant Director	**Gemma Aked-Priestley**
Production Manager	**Ian Taylor**
Stage Manager	**Laura Barton**
PR	**Freya Cowdry** for **Kate Morley PR**
Associate Producer	**Maya Ellis**

With thanks to:
Sibylla Wood, Jonathan Meth, Debbie Seymour,
The Diane Abbott Foundation, The Peggy Ramsay Foundation

This production first performed
Wednesday 9 January 2019 at Arcola Theatre, London

arcola
theatre

Munashe Chirisa
Akim

Theatre credits include: *Dr Faustus* (UK Tour), *Water, Bread and Salt* (UK Tour), All Of Us (UK Tour), *So You Think I'm Crazy* (Ovalhouse), *The Blue Room* (UK Tour).
Television credits include: *Zambezi News*.
Film credits include: *Time to Dance*.

Tyler Luke Cunningham
Lee

Theatre credits include: *Summer in London* (Stratford East), *The Butch Monologues* (UK Tour), *The Night Before Christmas* (Chickenshed).
Film & Television credits include: *Spider-Man Far From Home*, *Flack*, *Boy Meets Girl*.

David Kirkbride
Tone

Theatre credits include: *Under Milk Wood* (Northern Stage), *Pinocchio* (National Theatre), *The Crucible* (National UK Tour), *Rathband* (Tristan Bates Theatre), *Robin Hood and Marian* (New Vic Theatre), *Larksong* (Hoard Festival), *Unearthed* (Hoard Festival), *The Gift* (Hoard Festival), *Shrapnel: 34 Fragments of a Massacre* (Arcola Theatre), *The Muddy Choir* (Theatre Centre), *Luna Park* (The Albany), *Othello* (National Theatre), *Titus Andronicus* (Rep Theatre), *Voices of the Titanic*

(Vivid Theatre), *A Midsummer Night's Dream* (Roar Theatre), *The Machine Gunners* (Polka Theatre).
Television credits include: *The Spanish Princess*, *Doctors*, *Sherlock*, *Lodger*, *Emmerdale*, *Hetty Heather*, *Privates*, *Inspector George Gently*, *Silent Witness*, *Holby City*, *Steel River Blues*.
Film credits include: *Crooked House*, *Lady Macbeth*, *The Healer*, *Abschussfahrt*, *Zero Hour*.

Shaun Mason
Tel

Theatre credits include: *One Flew Over the Cuckoo's Nest* (Sheffield Crucible), *All's Well That Ends Well* (Globe), *Oliver Twist* (Regent's Park), *Black Lives Black Words* (Bush Theatre), *Romeo and Juliet* (Sheffield Crucible), *Feed the Beast* (Birmingham Rep Studio/Ipswich New Wolsey), *Peter Pan*, *Cinderella* (Liverpool Empire), *Clockwork Orange* (Glasgow Citizens Theatre), *Macbeth*, *Billy Wonderful* (Liverpool Everyman), *A Midsummer Night's Dream*, *Council Depot Blues* (Liverpool Royal Court), *Snow White* (St Helen's Theatre Royal).
Television credits include: *Trollied*, *Rellik*, *Snatch*, *Little Boy Blue*, *The Frankenstein Chronicles*, *Cilla*, *Luther*, *Scott & Bailey*, *Good Cop*, *Line of Duty*, *Shameless*, *Moving On*, *The Accused*.
Film credits include: *Kelly and Victor*, *Death Defying Acts*. Radio credits include: *A*

Christmas Carol, As You Like It, Once and Future King.

Jessye Romeo
Bev

Theatre credits include: *Big Guns* (The Yard), *The Islanders* (Whitechapel Gallery), *Itch and Scratch* (Hackney Showroom), *Martyr* (Unicorn/Bristol Old Vic/Traverse), *Our Days of Rage* (NYT), *Romeo and Juliet* (WAC Arts)
Television credits include: *Curfew*, *In The Long Run*, *Stan Lee's Lucky Man*, *Knowledge Seller*, *Will*.
Film credits include: *Mindhorn*, *The Somnambulists*.

Mehmet Ergen
Director

Mehmet Ergen is Artistic Director of Arcola Theatre.

His theatre credits for the company include *Richard III*, *Bliss*, *The Cherry Orchard*, *Drones, Baby, Drones*, *An Enemy of the People*, *The Cradle Will Rock*, *Clarion*, *Shrapnel: 34 Fragments of a Massacre*, *Don Gil of the Green Breeches*, *Mare Rider*, *Sweet Smell of Success*, *The Painter*, *Seven Deadly Sins* and *Macbeth*.

Other theatre credits include; *Fiddler on the Roof*, *Truth*, *Fool for Love*, *Betrayal*, *Ashes to Ashes*, *Water's Edge*, *Dumb Show*, *Lost in the Stars*, *Treemonisha*, *In The Jungle*

of the Cities, *Piano* and *King Lear*.

Ergen is also Artistic Director and founder of Talimhane Tiyatrosu in Istanbul and was previously Artistic Director of Southwark Playhouse, which he co-founded in 1993.

Gabriel Gbadamosi
Writer

Gabriel Gbadamosi is an Irish-Nigerian poet and playwright. *Stop and Search* is his play as a Londoner. His theatre credits include *Eshu's Faust* (Jesus College, Cambridge), *Hotel Orpheu* (Schaubühne, Berlin), *Shango* (DNA, Amsterdam); and for radio, *The Long, Hot Summer of '76* – winner of the first Richard Imison Award.

Gbadamosi's novel *Vauxhall* won the Tibor Jones Pageturner Prize and Best International Novel at the Sharjah Book Fair.

Eleanor Bull
Designer

In 2017 Eleanor won the Linbury Prize for Stage Design for Phoenix Dance Theatre's *Windrush: Movement of the People,* which is currently touring throughout the UK and Europe. Eleanor trained at Bristol Old Vic Theatre School, graduating with an MA in Theatre Design in 2017.

Theatrical Credits include:

American Idiot (Moutview), *The Directors' Festival 2018* (The Orange Tree), *Legacy* (The Egg, Theatre Royal Bath), *Isaac Came Home from the Mountain* (Theatre 503), *Windrush: Movement of the People* (West Yorkshire Playhouse), *Julius Caesar* (Bristol Old Vic Theatre), Crave (The Wardrobe, Bristol), *The Two Gentlemen of Verona* (The Redgrave Theatre, Bristol), *Othello* (Riverside Studios).

Richard Williamson
Lighting Designer

Richard frequently lights new writing and his most recent lighting and video designs include: *The Political History of Smack & Crack* (Edinburgh Festival & tour), *Bark! The Musical* (Swansong Productions), *Thor and Loki* (Vicky Graham Productions), *Lock and Key* and *I Have A Bad Feeling About This* (Vault Festival), *Beowulf,* (Unicorn Theatre), *Strangers In Between* (King's Head Theatre), *New Nigerians, Insignificance, Thebes Land* and *Drones, Baby, Drones,* (Arcola Theatre), *Boris: World King* (Trafalgar Studios), *The Body* (Barbican Centre); *Rotterdam,* (Trafalgar Studios, Theatre503 and New York). Other theatre credits include: *Great Expectations* (Tilted Wig), *Fiddler On The Roof,* (Istanbul),*Jason and the Argonauts* and *Septimus Bean and His Amazing Machine* (Unicorn Theatre), *Easter Rising* (Jermyn St Theatre), *Brenda* (High Tide and Yard Theatre), *Dusty* (Charing Cross Theatre), *Thrill Me – The Leopold and Loeb Story* (Greenwich Theatre, Edinburgh Festival & Climar Productions), *Shrapnel: 34 Fragments of a Massacre, Mare Rider* and *Happy Ending,* (Arcola Theatre), *La Trashiata, The Dispute, The Man Who Almost Killed Himself, Sleight and Hand* (Hibrow at Edinburgh Festival), *Ha Ha Holmes* (Jamie Wilson Productions).
Early lighting designs include: *Pied Piper* (Yard Theatre), *The Fu Manchu Complex,* (Ovalhouse Theatre), *Vieux Carre, Denial, Caritas* (King's Head Theatre); *The Last Session* (Tristan Bates Theatre), *The Dark Side of Love* (Roundhouse), *Amphibians* (Bridewell Theatre), *Richard III,* An *Arab Tragedy* (Swan Theatre Stratford and international tour), *20th Century Boy: The Musical* (New Wolsey Theatre; The Firewatchers (Old Red Lion), *The Taming of the Shrew, The Execution of Justice* and *Summer Begins* (Southwark Playhouse), *The Provoked Wife* (Greenwich Playhouse), *Thrill Me - The Leopold and Loeb Story* (Tristan Bates Theatre), *Boy With a Suitcase, Peer Gynt, Macbeth, A Midsummer Night's Dream, The Night Just Before the Forest, Tartuffe, Through a Cloud, King Arthur, Mojo, Mickybo, The Great Theatre of the World,*

Tombstone Tales and The Country (Arcola Theatre), *In My Name* (Trafalgar Studios), *Follow* (Finborough Theatre), *Play Size* (Young Vic).
Opera lighting includes: B*allo - A Masked Ball* & *Tosca* (King's Head Theatre) and *La Boheme* and *The Mikado* (Charing Cross Theatre).
Seasonal productions include *A Christmas Carol* (Seabright Productions) and regular pantomimes for Evolution Productions.
Richard is Production Manager for C venues at the Edinburgh Festival, Technical Manager for the Greenwich and Docklands Festivals and develops industry iOS applications such as PlayFadePause and Rosco's myGobo.

Richard's gallery and full CV can be seen at www.richard-williamson.com

Daniel Balfour
Sound Designer

Theatre Includes: *Blood Wedding* (Omnibus Theatre), *LAVA* (Nottingham Playhouse), *Effigies Of Wickedness* (The Gate), *Great Apes*, *I Call My Brothers*, *Caught* (Arcola Theatre), *VINOVAT -Ä* (Teatru Replica, Bucharest), *#Dracula* (The Curve); *Seafret* (Old Red Lion, HighTide), *Figures Of Speech-Series* (Almeida Theatre); *Great Expectations* (Merton Arts Space), *Spindrift* (Theatre Royal Plymouth), *RE: Home* (Yard Theatre), *DREAM*, *Jenufa–Opera Works*

(ENO), *Walking the Tightrope* (Theatre Delicatessen), *SOLO* (Bush Theatre); *Nude* (Hope Theatre), *Deathwatch* (Roundhouse); *The Dumb Waiter*, *Woyczek* (Old Nick Theatre).
Theatre as Associate Includes: *We Are Here* (La Mama, NY), *Fanny & Alexander*, *The Lorax-Toronto Tour* (The Old Vic), *People Places & Things* (Headlong UK Tour), *Life Of Galileo* (Young Vic), *Oresteia* (Almeida Theatre), *Frogman* (Traverse Theatre), *Sex With Strangers* (Hampstead Theatre), *Disco Pigs* (Uk Tour); *How I Hacked My Way Into Space* (Unlimited Theatre).

Dan trained at the Royal Central School of Speech and Drama.

Gemma Aked-Priestley
Assistant Director

Directing credits include *Passing* (Staged Reading, Theatre Royal Haymarket/ Royal Academy of Dramatic Arts/The Bunker Theatre/ Pleasance Theatre), *My Dad's Blind* (Winner of Best Production, Dublin Fringe Festival 2018); the European premiere of *Gracie* (Finborough Theatre); *Grimm: An Untold Tale* (Underbelly, the Edinburgh Fringe Festival) and *Tender Napalm* (Karamel Club, Mountview Academy of Theatre Arts).
Assistant Direction credits includes Sam Hodges on the world premiere and revival

of Howard Brenton's *The Shadow Factory* (Nuffield Southampton Theatres); Daniel Goldman on *Thebes Land* (Arcola Theatre); David Mercatali on *Tonight With Donny Stixx* (The Bunker Theatre) and Matt Cowart on *Lockhart: A New Southern Gothic Musical* (Bernie Grant Arts Centre).

From 2016-2017 she was the Assistant Director for The Mono Box where she co-founded PLAYSTART.

In 2017 and 2018 Gemma supported Jill Green Casting with auditions for the National Theatre's UK tour of *War Horse*. In the summer of 2017 Gemma shadowed *War Horse* rehearsals in London and Canterbury. Gemma studied at the University of East Anglia and trained at Mountview Academy of Theatre Arts.

She is the recipient of bursaries from the Mayflower Theatre, Yorkshire Ladies Council of Education, Barker-Mill Foundation and the JMK Trust.

Laura Barton
Stage Manager

Trained at Central School of Speech and Drama.

She worked for English National Opera for five years before moving on to work at Garsington Opera,

Opera North and The Royal Opera House. She toured the UK with the *Rent- 20th Anniversary Tour* and travelled to Australia and around England with *Orpheus: a Gypsy Jazz musical* Co Produced by Battersea Arts Centre.

Recent work includes *Cabaret* with English Theatre Frankfurt and 'The Return of Ulysses' with Opera Collective Ireland. In the new year Laura will be Stage Managing for the Royal Opera House, Linbury Studio.

Ian Taylor for eStage
Production Manager

Trained at Guildhall School of Music and Drama.

Founded in 2014, eStage provides theatre and event production services for the entertainment industry through its team of experienced production managers, builders, artists and technicians.

Theatre includes *New Nigerians*, *The Plague*, *Not Talking*, *The Blue Hour of Natalie Barney*, *Thebes Land*, *The Cherry Orchard*, *The Lower Depths*, *After Independence*, *The Island Nation*, *Werther*, *Pelléas et Mélisande* and *Il Tabarro* (Arcola Theatre), *The Dreamers* (Abbey Road), *Schism* (Park Theatre), *Giulio Cesare* and *Così fan tutte* (Bury Court Opera), *Hanna* (Arcola Theatre and National Tour), *The Funeral*

Director, *Trestle*, *Diary of a Teenage Girl*, *Orca* and *Tomcat* (Southwark Playhouse), *Shadowtracks*, *The Cutlass Crew*, *The Price*, *Deep Waters*, *The Fizz* and *Eliza and the Swans* (W11 Opera), *L'Agrippina* (The Barber Institute of Fine Arts, University of Birmingham), *Our House* (National Tour), *Whisper House* (The Other Palace), *Oedipus Rex* and *L'Enfant et Les Sortilèges* (The Philharmonia Orchestra at Royal Festival Hall), *The Man Who Would Be King*, *Peter Pan* and *Red Riding Hood* (Greenwich Theatre), *Vanities: The Musical* (Trafalgar Studios), *Who Framed Roger Rabbit?* (Future Cinema), *Jack and the Beanstalk*, *Snow White*, *Cinderella* and *Aladdin* (Upstage Productions).

Maya Ellis
Associate Producer

Maya Ellis is a theatre producer. Her credits include Whalebone and Moonfleece (Edinburgh Festival Fringe). She has also worked for multiple venues including Arcola Theatre, Theatre503, Finborough Theatre, Ovalhouse and the Southbank Centre.

Maya Ellis currently works for Summerhall in Edinburgh and the award-winning company Clean Break.

KILN THEATRE

THE TRICYCLE TRANSFORMED

TICKETS FROM
£10

KAMMY DARWEISH   RINA FATANIA

KARAN GILL   NICHOLAS KHAN

NICHOLAS PRASAD   MAANUV THIARA

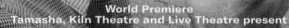

World Premiere
Tamasha, Kiln Theatre and Live Theatre present

APPROACHING EMPTY

by Ishy Din
directed by Pooja Ghai

9 JAN – 2 FEB 2019

 @KilnTheatre

Kiln Theatre, 269 Kilburn High Road, London, NW6 7JR

Brent

ARTS COUNCIL
ENGLAND

Registration No. 1396429
Charity No. 276892

**arcola
theatre**

Arcola Theatre is one of London's leading off-West End theatres.

Locally engaged and internationally minded, we stage a diverse programme of plays, operas and musicals. New productions from major artists appear alongside cutting-edge work from the most exciting emerging companies.

Every year, our Participation department creates over 13,500 creative opportunities for the people of Hackney and beyond, and 26 weeks of free rehearsal space for theatre artists of colour. Our pioneering environmental initiatives are internationally renowned, and aim to make Arcola the world's first carbon-neutral theatre.

MAKE THIS HAPPEN   Text ARCO14 £3 to 70070
to give £3 in support of Arcola   Standard network charges apply.

Artistic Director **Mehmet Ergen**	Executive Producer **Leyla Nazli**		Executive Director **Ben Todd**
Associate Director **Jack Gamble**	Technical Manager **Geoff Hense**	Participation Manager **Bec Martin-Williams**	Assistant Producer **Richard Speir**
Marketing Manager **Maddy Breen**	Front of House & Box Office Manager **Norna Yau**	Operations Manager **Natalja Derendiajeva**	Bar Manager **Trystan Kent**
Finance Assistant **Steve Haygreen**	Assistant Bar Manager **Gabriel Jones**	Assistant Technical Manager **Michael Paget**	Digital Marketing Officer **Ankesh Shah**
Participation Coordinator **Rach Skyer**	Software Developers **Nick Cripps, Martin Poot**	Health & Safety Manager **Charlotte Croft**	New Work Assistant **Eleanor Dawson**
Sustainability Assistant **Helen Freudenberg**	Individual Giving & Development **Lora Krasteva**	Front of House Supervisors **Emily Jones Mary Roubos James York**	Cleaner **Suber Kemal Sabit**

For a full staff list please see **arcolatheatre.com/staff**   *With special thanks to our volunteers and Supporters*

Game Changers
Graham and Christine Benson, Roger Bradburn & Helen Main,
Andrew Cripps, Robert Fowler, Daniel Friel,
David Alan & Jean Grier, Sarah Morrison, Rosie Schumm

Trailblazers
Katie Bradford, Catrin Evans,
Gold Family, Jon Gilmartin, Stuart Honey,
Melanie Johnson, Katrin Maeurich

 ARTS COUNCIL ENGLAND   **⊢Hackney**   **Bloomberg**   **phf** Paul Hamlyn Foundation

www.arcolatheatre.com   **020 7503 1646**

STOP AND SEARCH

Gabriel Gbadamosi

STOP AND SEARCH

OBERON BOOKS
LONDON

WWW.OBERONBOOKS.COM

First published in 2019 by Oberon Books Ltd
521 Caledonian Road, London N7 9RH
Tel: +44 (0) 20 7607 3637 / Fax: +44 (0) 20 7607 3629
e-mail: info@oberonbooks.com
www.oberonbooks.com

Visit www.oberonbooks.com to read more about all our books and to buy them. You will
also find features, author interviews and news of any author events, and you can sign up for
e-newsletters so that you're always first to hear about our new releases.

Director's Note:

If we can see the ghost in the first scene,
you can do this play.

SCENE ONE
ANYONE CAN GO

Driving in the car, TEL, a white guy, and AKIM, an African, stand on stage, motorway music far and spacy, the back seat and boot space behind piled up with domed beaver hats. The two men silent, uncomfortable, shifting from one foot to the other: the driver, TEL, appalled, judgmental; the passenger, AKIM, embarrassed, dripping wet. It's a long journey, so like that for a long time…

… The beat of the music skips and travels, gives us time and space to imagine who these men are, make up our minds about them, come back to notice the half-empty coke bottle on the floor, wonder what's going on… AKIM will be trying to ease out of his wet things unobtrusively, one at a time – back pack, coat sleeve, shirts, shoulder strap – one shoe on, one sock off – his stuff a gathering puddle at his feet over the time of the scene.

TEL signals with a hand across his throat to cut the music – it snaps down not off.

TEL: Let me tell you the rules.

Stop dripping in the fucking car.

See I'm trying 'a drive.

We're not stopping, so piss in the bottle. When it's full – *you fucking spill it* – fling it out.

That's for starters.

Fucking hell.

(AKIM nods and nods…)

Who you nodding at?

AKIM: Thank you.

(TEL gives him a funny look.)

TEL: Where you from?

AKIM: UK.

TEL: *UK?* Who the fuck says they're from *UK*?

AKIM: It's OK. Just as far as we can go.

TEL: You got a passport?

AKIM: Yes sah, I have my passport here.

(AKIM fumbles under his belt, struggles to get out a water-tight plastic bag, a long job to undo elastic bands and get to the passport.)

TEL: Nah, it's not my problem.

AKIM: *(Scans TEL's face anxiously.)* No?

TEL: You got your problems, I got mine.

(AKIM thinks and starts to fold the bag away.)

Under the fucking Alps.

I'm not going in another tunnel, come Calais I'm getting the boat.

Mountain on top of yer, it's not right. What am I, a fucking dwarf?

I got my hands sweating.

AKIM: Anywhere you can take me.

TEL: The other end of this tunnel. Don't fucking annoy me.

(AKIM nodding. TEL gives him another funny look.)

At least from the boat you can make a swim for it.

You see 'em swim the Channel. You seen that?

(AKIM shrugs, he doesn't know.)

8

Yeah, they swim it.

Covered in fat. Trying not to get knocked down by a tanker.

Fucking sweat, I'm fucking drowning in it.

AKIM: Slow down.

(TEL looks up sharply, flinches and slows down with his hand out, palm forward.)

TEL: … You're gonna keep me awake.

AKIM: What?

TEL: See that car in front? Almost touch it?

That was a long way off last time I looked.

Just talk to me. Don't fall asleep.

Make me talk back.

(AKIM looks how you would if that was you.)

How long you been standing there?

AKIM: … Not long.

TEL: In the rain?

It's alright, you don't have to tell me. I saw you jump up when you saw my number plates, rain bouncing off yer hood.

Lucked out, n't yer?

Mont Blanc mountain on top of yer. You're dry now.

But you ain't home.

So keep talking. That's why I've picked yer.

(TEL clocks AKIM frozen, staring ahead into the tunnel.)

Cos you looked miserable.

AKIM: I'm so sorry.

TEL: Least I won't have to stomach some cheerful fucking Johnny on about his holiday.

I'd have chucked him out the car. And you can see I ain't stopping.

You smoke?

AKIM: No.

TEL: Crack a window your side. Don't want a crick in my neck.

(TEL leans back to fumble for his fags in the pocket of his coat.)

You illegal, innit?

AKIM: You can drop me after the tunnel.

TEL: Said you wanted to get to London. I said get in. What's the problem?

Where's my fags?

AKIM: You are too near the wall.

(TEL straightens up, both hands back on the front of his thighs. He carefully wipes down one after the other on his trousers.)

TEL: My hands wet. Get out a fag and light it.

It's like pressure on yer head, n't it?

(AKIM, eyes on the road, gets out cigarettes and lighter from the coat pocket, hands trembling he makes to put one in his mouth.)

Not with your spit on it!

I don't fucking know where you've been!

AKIM: Please, control the car.

TEL: … Stop shaking. Hold yer hands still, light it.

AKIM: Wait, until we come out.

(TEL gives a funny look.)

TEL: … Yeah, probably.

You get tunnel vision, dn't yer? All them lights going over.

Walls close in. Yer eyes wobble.

What's this? It going deeper?

AKIM: It's not going down. Cars are still coming. See?
It's OK. I'm here. Keep going.

(Pause.)

TEL: You believe that? What is it, a mind trick?

AKIM: You can wait. So I know. You can control the car.

(The cigarettes go invisibly back into the coat pocket, unobserved.)

TEL: Yeah.

Keep talking like that. Keep going.

Come a long way?

What's your story?

AKIM: What God gives me.

TEL: *God?*

What, you got a bomb?

Not in my fucking car.

AKIM: Excuse me?

TEL: Fucking God?

Let's just get through the fucking tunnel.

I'm not dying in no fucking cave for no fucking God. You can –

AKIM: Please, language.

TEL: What?

AKIM: It's too much. I can't follow. I just see the wrong thing. Speak so I can follow.

TEL: You a muslim?

What's your name?

AKIM: Akim.

TEL: What's that, muslim?

AKIM: You can call me George.

TEL: … Listen, Joe – no names, I don't wanna know your fucking name – I'm gonna call you Harry – I don't want God in my car when I'm driving through a tunnel. Nothing personal. I been up non-stop. I ain't got time for that. Y'get me? I'm busy. Gotta get back. It's a lot to do. And I don't want no one looking over my shoulder.

It ain't over, and it ain't gonna end in no fucking tunnel.

AKIM: Go on.

TEL: Go on, what?

AKIM: Keep talking. It's better.

TEL: I'm not going on, you go on. That's your job.

AKIM: … I have a question.

TEL: Go on.

AKIM: How long now can you go on no sleep? We can't just stop?

Come out of the tunnel, you just have to go under and come back up.

TEL: And find you've fucked off with the car?

What you take me for? Fucking take off – with all this in the back.

AKIM: Eh-heh. And who are all these people?

TEL: What people?

(AKIM glances over his shoulder.)

Them hats – that's beaver. Bought 'em 50 quid each, I can sell 'em hundred and fifty down Deptford. That's what's paying for all this.

AKIM: You are rushing them to market?

TEL: And, anyway, what d'you wanna know for?

AKIM: What's the rush?

TEL: I gotta get on that ferry tonight.

AKIM: I won't steal. They won't spoil. Please, can we slow down?

TEL: Nah, you're not getting me, bruv. I got contacts. Sell this lot off one go. Those old Rastas'll have 'em. They ain't going out of fashion. They can get their hair up inside. And they got the good weed, they're rolling in it.

Nah, I gotta get back before she wakes up.

Gonna catch her out. She won't be expecting it. I only left yesterday. Be a surprise. She gets up in the morning, I'll be there, non-fucking-stop.

She been playing me, I'll find out. I find a man there, I'll fucking take his eyes out.

(Gives AKIM a funny look.)

Don't be telling no one that's beaver. It's rabbit. Beaver's illegal. Like you.

Getting up in my business. What fucking business is it of yours?

Who wants to know?

AKIM: Like you, I'm just trying to find what's going on.

TEL: Nothing's going on.

What d'you think's going on?

AKIM: Import-export. Is that not so? You are doing your work.

TEL: Doing my –? What d'you think I do? Mind yer fucking business.

AKIM: … There's light at the end of this tunnel.

TEL: What fucking tunnel? You're the one sticking his nose in. You can't see the big flashing sign saying *Keep Out*?

You don't wanna know what I do.

I'm doing what I'm doing. That's what I do.

I don't wanna know what you're up to.

AKIM: Look. It's coming.

(Pause – their eyes open out from the tunnel.)

TEL: … What a relief.

Got through that.

AKIM: I thank my eyes to have come this far.

TEL: … Sight for sore eyes?

You speak funny.

Speak English.

You'll need it.

AKIM: The border is here?

TEL: France, n't it?

(AKIM fumbles for the bundle under his belt.)

AKIM: They're checking?

TEL: Nah, look at the queues. It's the other side. Going in.

They just want yer money – use the tunnel.

Rob you on the way in. Italians rob you on the way out.

See that wop back there in his glass box – saw you jump in – stare up my money like it ain't no good. Stare up my car like it's stolen.

What? *It's my car. Take the fucking money.* Stare at me like a fucking foreign monkey.

(Pause.)

Where's yours?

Where's yer money? You got any?

What you got?

(AKIM reaches into his pocket, shows coins.)

What? Cheeky bastard.

Bum a lift all the way? What about petrol?

What's in yer other pockets? Euros?

AKIM: No.

TEL: Cheeky fucker.

> Now you can breathe you wanna tell me you're trying to sneak a lift all the way.

AKIM: You can drop me.

TEL: Lesson One. Pay yer way.

> What fucking use is that? No money. How you gonna get across? Swim?

> You *better* fucking earn it.

AKIM: Rain has stopped.

TEL: You got a fucking nerve.

> What else you got?

> I'm telling you now – you got anything, you better swallow it, or chuck it out the window.

> They always stop me.

> … What's in yer bag?

AKIM: *(Holds up the coins.)* I can offer one coffee, I don't drink.

> *(TEL looks, relents and shakes his head.)*

TEL: I'm not stopping. I gotta be on that ferry.

You got anything, get rid of it.

You'll get searched.

AKIM: I don't know drugs.

TEL: I'm just saying. Maybe you think you've got balls.

> Them dogs'll have 'em off yer.

Don't take the risk.

AKIM: … How can we go forward, and be safe? And you are sleeping?

TEL: You think I'm on drugs?

AKIM: You don't need coffee?

TEL: Nah, I only missed one night. Yesterday. London-Monte Carlo.

My girlfriend's a croupier. I had to go there.

She didn't get no sleep, neither. I'm trying to get her pregnant.

She better be, I put in the work.

AKIM: So… from there you are rushing back?

TEL: Home? Nah, I had to stop in Milan pick up these in the back.

London-Monte Carlo. Monte Carlo-Milan, this morning. Pick you up at the tunnel-back to London.

She been acting funny.

AKIM: The group… something?

TEL: … In the casinos. *Croupier*. Turn the tables on yer.

She better not.

Nah, not her. She don't matter. She gotta be pregnant first.

And it's gotta be mine.

I'm not talking her – it's *my* woman, Bev – *Beverley*. Sitting home – back in London. Her.

She *not* pregnant, that's the problem.

She telling me, *Oh, no, it's alright.* Like it's my fucking fault and it was hers.

I'm rubbing one out in the hospital – grubby mag – grubby me – and she saying, *Maybe we can do IVF.* But that ain't what comes back.

Fucking grief.

Now she wants to kick me out. It's me, I've done something to her. It's my fault she can't fucking breed.

That ain't right. Is it right? I should have no fucking chance cos she don't?

... Telling me get out.

I got a right. I ain't going nowhere.

She loves me, like that means I can't have no kids.

How's that gonna work?

Can't have no kids, she's gotta let me go.

Knock me down, stand me up. Knock me down again.

Like she's standing in my way, she loves me, and I'm supposed to punch her in the belly? What's that?

We been going out since school. Where'm I going?

Come home, find her sneaking round on the phone, she gotta go out – *Where you going?*

It's my business, I can go out if I want, it's a free country.

I let it go.

Come back, she's shivering on the bed like the floor's hit her and she can't get up.

Course it's fucking hit her, but what about me?

You're free, you can do what you want, Tel.

Yeah, I gotta try, but now she wants to start fucking about?

She's gotta give me a chance.

(TEL glances for answer at AKIM)

AKIM: I see.

TEL: What?

AKIM: What you are saying.

TEL: I've said what I'm fucking saying. What am I supposed to do?

AKIM: … See how the road turns. We are still coming down the mountain. We have to take the road steady. Make sure the brakes are working.

TEL: What you fucking on about?

AKIM: We have to calm down.

TEL: Calm down? And she wants me to fucking slap her?

I ain't laid a finger on that gel. And she telling everyone I have.

What about that?

AKIM: I don't know.

(Pause.)

TEL: There… there… feel that? Course the fucking brakes work. Costs a fortune.

Nice car, n't it? Fast.

I'm not gonna do this in a banger.

Merc – S class. Hire bloke's telling me he don't want 'em after they done 10. Well, I put 3,000 on the clock for him.

You weren't supposed to go out the country!

Fuck him. I want a shag, I'll get a room.

I'm paying for it.

He's paying for it.

Them in the back, they're paying for it.

Go where I want. Who's to know?

Treat me like I got off the bus. Shit on his shoes, stink up his seats.

Wave the cash under his nose, thick fucking wodge, he's tearing his jacket off, rolling up his sleeves like he's Superman, bragging he only does top of the range.

Money talks. Must be why you don't.

Look at ya. Course you don't fucking know.

(Heavy sigh.) Poor as fuck.

(AKIM leans forward and picks up the swilling plastic coke bottle.)

AKIM: I know now it's not your car.

TEL: You wouldn't be in it if it was. Course it's not my fucking car. Look in the mirror. Who let you in?

'Scuse me while you piss.

AKIM: I don't want.

(AKIM places the bottle behind.)

TEL: There's gonna be a layby coming up, before the motorway. You got a choice, you wanna come or not?

I'm going, I'm not stopping.

AKIM: … It's very chanceful.

TEL: Life, n't it?

Take it as it comes.

Get in the fast lane, or get out and walk.

Look at you. You stink. What you got to lose?

You got any kids?

AKIM: … Not anymore.

(TEL glances across, and says nothing.)

TEL: … Rough, n't it?

(AKIM glances at TEL, and looks down.)

You never know, though, do yer?

What if there's kids out there you don't know about?
Running round, and they never told yer?

That's what's kept 'em safe. Nothing to do with you.

You see 'em in a shop, they take yer money, give it to
someone else. Don't even know you're alive.

Can't kill 'em off cos you can't get hold of 'em.

Can't even see what they look like.

Could be anyone. Round that age. – Or that one.

There's been a few didn't keep track of.

You see a kid, you look round for the mum.

But you didn't wanna know then.

Now you do.

You see 'em pour out the playground – and you feel like a ghost.

All that jumping and running and singing –

AKIM: *(Shakes his head.)* Don't bandage your head before it's broken.

We still can get through.

(TEL looks at AKIM and frowns.)

TEL: Well, you woke up.

What put you on the planet?

AKIM: I'm thinking ahead.

You don't know me. I don't know you.

Passport check is there.

You will say, *I don't know who's in the car…?*

TEL: Depends. If it comes to that.

It comes on top, it's everyone for his self, n't it?

(AKIM frowns, not getting it.)

I just give him a lift. You looked at his passport. N't that right, officer?

(Now he gets it.)

Whoa! Hold on, not so fucking fast. What makes you think I'm letting you on board and you ain't got a pot to piss in?

You're taking the piss.

Fucking liberty.

AKIM: You are a good man, doing your best.

(TEL looks at AKIM, taken aback, and out at the road, fighting with himself.)

TEL: ... Well, yeah, fuck it, why not?

What's it say on the passport? Let's have a look.

(AKIM gets it out – a long job.)

Don't let 'em see it come out a' that. You have to swim, that's not gonna keep you afloat.

(AKIM opens it to the photo, TEL glances.)

Don't look nothing like yer. Grow a beard.

How much that cost?

AKIM: Please...

TEL: What d'you want?

AKIM: I want to know if I can cross.

TEL: There's too many of yer. *Fuck off.*

AKIM: What's wrong? I have my passport here.

TEL: I'm not looking at it. I'm looking at you. *Safe home.*

See how it works?

AKIM: I don't see.

TEL: You're not coming in.

I don't believe yer.

AKIM: You don't believe?

TEL: Simple.

AKIM: So?

I have to pass. Through you?

TEL: Border police.

But you ain't got a story together, have yer?

Where've you lived in London?

AKIM: … Here and there.

TEL: See?

It's not me, it's you standing in your way.

What happened to him in there? How d'you get his passport?

AKIM: … We are playing here?

TEL: *(Shrugs.)* If you want.

AKIM: Just fooling around…

TEL: … Don't judge me, bruv.

I'm helping you. I'm giving you one a' them hats to wear, that's how much you cost.

For all I know, you done him in and took it.

You're on the run. You could be anyone.

(AKIM slowly nods.)

What, you gonna pull a knife?

Cos I fingered yer?

You better think again the speed you're going.

You won't make it.

AKIM: I won't?

TEL: Not in a fucking million years.

Not with a face like that.

Right now, you're saying you wanna limp into London with a bundle on yer back and a couple a' coins.

It ain't paved with gold, y'know.

Make it fucking real.

What you worth? Who the fuck are you to come in?

AKIM: *(Points at the page.)* It says *Born*, London. Not *Died* anywhere.

TEL: *Bandage my head.* That's a good one.

Except it ain't my head that's broken.

Is it?

(Pause. AKIM folds the passport away under his belt.)

AKIM: … Water was coming up. People were crying…

TEL: Now we're getting somewhere.

AKIM: The boat was not steady… They said that one to us. Those bastards. *Don't bandage your head…*

TEL: … I'm listening.

AKIM: I'm ready to die anywhere here on this road.

(TEL stiffens.)

The man in there is dead.

If we crash now, I can't care.

How many times can one man die?

I can die as him.

The body is there – who knows?

Who cares who is there, who is not there?

I thank him, I can go.

At least I can say I tried.

I congratulate myself as a man that I tried.

TEL: … Fucking had me going there…

He's dead, what killed him?

AKIM: His time had come.

TEL: … You got his passport.

AKIM: Death has no passport – anyone can go.

Any time.

He took the chance.

(TEL shakes his head awake.)

TEL: Will yer stop going on like we're gonna crash? I can
handle myself – I can handle a car with blue fucking
flashing sirens after it.

It's not a fucking boat.

And it ain't fucking overloaded neither.

(AKIM turns round to the hats, lifts one onto his head.)

What you doing?

AKIM: *(Looking.)* The eyes will follow you.

You can't save people in the water. And they know.

They can see they will drown.

You can't help them.

They are just looking – who will hold them now?

Looking at you – and drowning.

The eyes of anyone you have ever lost, who was depending on you.

(Pause.)

TEL: Take it off.

Take it off – don't get the fucking hat wet.

(AKIM lifts the hat back onto the pile.)

AKIM: The calling stops.

Just heavy sheets of water folding over them.

They've gone.

(Pause. TEL glances across – and again – and again.)

TEL: Wouldn't like to meet you on a dark night.

(AKIM wipes his face clean with his hand.)

AKIM: Just playing.

(TEL's jaw drop.)

You are not sleeping now. And we are closer ever than before.

Let's go.

TEL: … You mean I been fucking done?

(AKIM doesn't get it.)

None a' that's true?

AKIM: *(Shrugs.)* You want to know everything, and you can't know.

It's not for you.

TEL: It's *my* fucking car…

(AKIM looks at him.)

…*ish.*

You lost your kids. And you still grab someone's passport?

What the fuck?

There it is floating – people going under, fucking kids – and you still want it?

What's that? Fuck is it true or not – who does that?

What for?

AKIM: They died in fire.

I can get more.

(Pause.)

TEL: You're right, I don't wanna fucking know.

Keep it to yourself.

It's give me a bad feeling.

(Pause.)

AKIM: You want children – where you can have them live – and nothing will stop you.

(Pause.)

Is that not so?

(Pause.)

TEL: That don't make you a good man.

AKIM: You are judging me?

(Pause.)

TEL: You can't hear it – it's in my head – that's the fucking brakes going on.

You're mental.

Trying to get up inside my head.

I've let you get too close.

You're playing me.

Fucking kids, my arse.

You been listening – clocking me – What, you fucking trying me on for size?

Change yer fucking passport?

You think they don't look?

AKIM: … I can hear your mind running. One plus two making four.

We want the same thing – to live.

TEL: Yeah, well, then no fucking ghost stories.

Looking in my head.

Get the fuck out.

AKIM: I'm not there.

(TEL gives him a funny look.)

TEL: … Too fucking close.

Y'don't know who yer dealing with.

I was you, I'd stick with that one.

AKIM: *(Shrugs.)* I have my own passport.

You don't want to believe.

(Pause.)

TEL: Trying 'a fucking scam me?

Fucking get more kids.

Sweat in yer own skin.

Fucking animal.

That dog – over the wall – looks at me, beady eyes – knows what I'm thinking before I do. I growl at it. Make it go berserk. But that's alright, there's that wall.

That's why they got you shut out.

You all look on the telly like you could do damage. Dirty, dangerous pack a dogs the lot a' ya.

AKIM: … Now I'm a dog?

TEL: *Woof!*

(AKIM shakes his head and throws up his arms.)

AKIM: And you want me to play along?

TEL: Get down on your knees and beg, y'cunt. You're getting off.

AKIM: I won't beg.

Layby is coming, you can drop me.

(Silence between them.)

TEL: That's it, play dead.

You – you haven't got a fucking hope.

Wanna know who I am? I'm your worst fucking nightmare.

You won't see it – be splashed all over the fucking papers tomorrow. I'm the one who planned it, the biggest fucking robbery this side of fifty-three million. A fucking spectacular.

Yeah, that's right, I'm a fucking robber.

Who you gonna tell?

Try an' rob me, y'cunt.

You don't fucking know me.

No one does.

I'm not even in the country.

And I got the receipts to prove it, cos I pay my fucking bills.

All you see's a fat fucking tourist – fat fuck off Merc – running round for a shag. Cos I got it *planned* I won't be there. Nowhere near no robbery. I'm in Milan, buying them in the back.

Bite my fucking arse.

Saw your chance, dn't yer?

Cos I'm busy getting the fucking girl pregnant and there's kids washing up on the beach, you can get in there under my skin.

You don't know me.

I got fucking morals.

You climb back in your fucking ditch.

You're dead in the water.

I don't take shit. And I'm not taking you.

(AKIM starts to gather and pull on his wet stuff.)

AKIM: Dead in the water.

> You don't know.
>
> You won't know – That struggle with your cloths.
>
> How long –

TEL: *(Sticks up two fingers.)* Read that sign? Two fucking minutes.

AKIM: … before we wake up dead on the road?

TEL: That don't matter, you're already dead, n't yer?

AKIM: Yes.

(Pause – TEL looks at AKIM for more. Nothing comes.)

TEL: Shut up.

> Why me?
>
> What's that mean?

AKIM: People die in water – and they die on the road.

> It means you can slow down.
>
> Don't die from fear.
>
> If you want to know, the driver lost control…

(AKIM and TEL look at each other.)

> There was fire. The tanker crashed and spilled oil over the road.
>
> Many people died.
>
> The children. And the mother.
>
> I was not there.

After that one, you too, you are dead.

My life ended then.

(AKIM stops struggling with his clothes.)

You can't move on.

You have to run. And keep running.

How I move I don't care.

I will get there.

TEL: ... You didn't fucking drown.

AKIM: Everyone drowns.

People going under – you won't sleep – but still you wake up, cold and sweating.

You want them back. No one ever comes.

You drown with them.

And never stop.

(Pause.)

TEL: Sorry about that.

AKIM: ... Please, I just want to drop.

TEL: Yeah, you said.

Maybe I am a bit tired.

Bit on edge. Got off on the wrong leg.

Lot going on.

Woman fucking hates me.

Trying 'a scrape a living. Make a fucking change.

And for what?

Long way to go, n't it? Before you get there. Tunnel all the way.

Pinholes for eyes.

Fucking burnt out.

And it's all in French.

Miles and miles of fucking kilometres.

Go on, take the wheel.

I gotta stretch me legs.

(The music stops; TEL steps aside. AKIM jumps with fright.)

'Course we fucking stopped.

(TEL waves the car key.)

Pulled over you still didn't wake up.

You fell asleep, y'cunt.

And you snore.

(TEL waves him away.)

Go on, get out. I'm locking it. And your stuff.

(AKIM steps out with his bundle of belongings.)

Piss over that way.

(AKIM moves off, pulling his clothes on, with his back to TEL)

*

(TEL gets out a fag, faces out front – his eyes scanning and following the fast flow of traffic. Props up the back of his ear with a finger – summoning the sounds of cars flashing past.)

TEL: What d'you reckon?

Come on, I can take it. Is he for fucking real, or what?

He's obviously fucking lying. Look at him, wet and slippery, like a fucking eel. Course it's not his passport.

Let him get a word in edgeways, what's he gonna say next?

Keeps you awake, though, dn't it?

Let him come?

What's not illegal? Even having a smoke.

Un-be-fucking-lievable.

He ain't gonna go the police, is he?

What's he got, number plates? He don't know fuck.

Let him lie – no skin off my nose.

Drop him off at the boat, he can float under his own steam.

He don't get in the French can have him. Let him lie his way out a' that. *Can't stop, running from the Foreign Legion.*

They catch him, that's five years in prison.

Better not fuck up.

Foreign fucking prison. They still break rocks.

It don't look good for him, does it?

(Shrugs.) It's not my business.

(Pointed out front.) None a' *you* stopping.

(His eyes slide sideways.)

Slow it down, that's going a bit fast. Who's after you? Make sure you get home, she don't want it that bad.

The rest a' yer fucking dreaming, don't wanna get there. Stick in low gear you won't have to get home and face it.

Too fucking late.

You weren't there.

Got the time wrong. And you drive on the wrong fucking side. Down the wrong end of a fucking tunnel.

… I gotta get back.

Look at me, shivering – middle a' nowhere.

(Glances round at AKIM.)

He slowing me down, or it's just the stuff wearing off?

Anyway, what am I, a people carrier? I got a life – fast fucking Merc, I'm busy.

Stand out in the fucking cold.

That's his job.

Get in the way. Fucking ghost, half dead, trying 'a flag down the traffic – turns out a bit a cardboard blowing about on the road.

They're everywhere – clumps of 'em like fucking weeds. Like they grow there. Then you see the stragglers – and you think *Fuck me, are they still people?* Cardboard shifters getting swallowed up in the windscreen and you don't wanna look back how their life just stopped.

I had to pick him. – He was there.

Look what I got.

… Lie like he fucking wants, don't get me involved.

They come pouring in.

They all fucking come through fire and water, dn't they?
Still got legs.

I'm done being me, I'll go over there.

Let 'em in, the fucking story changes – they wanna move
into your house, your fucking job, your socks.

I didn't vote for that.

Didn't fucking vote.

It's their problem, they run the country, they can sort it
out

(Glances again.)

No home. No fucking money.

Come legging it – on water. Dead kids on yer back. Holes
in yer fucking socks. Should have fucking sorted it.

Let him walk. See how far he gets.

(Lights that cigarette.)

Lose yer woman in fire.

You lit the fucking match. It's *you* – living like you fucking
do.

Set the world on fire – now you gotta run.

You *let* her go.

You don't blow up the fucking world and wonder where
it's gone.

Wondering why you got no kids.

(Smokes.)

What of it?

Just un-fucking-lucky.

No kids. Happen to anyone.

… It's hit her, though. Acting all funny.

Who she seeing?

Turns round, tells me, *We're the lucky ones.* The lucky ones.

We got our lives. Yeah? *Look at the refugees.*

Like that's alright, fill up the bloody country with foreigners. *Come off it, Bev.*

No, she says, *you can't stop them. They're coming – they have to. All you can do is slow it down. Change how you feel about it.*

I said she shouldn't have fucking gone to College.

Gonna have kids but you found out what a bad fucking world it is?

That's why they never come.

Fucking stress.

Have to carry that round like a donkey.

… It's her own fault.

Put on *that* fucking weight? – She didn't have to!

She got it out a' me.

Man's got business. I'm doing it for her. That's all she has to know.

38

Can't give her kids, gotta give her money.

The other one, I give her kids – I gotta give her money.

I got to get the fucking money, n't it?

For her.

What's it matter some little girl she don't know's pregnant?

I'll deal with that as it comes.

Come to that... let it fucking tear me apart. I'm not leaving. She can't make me.

It's my kid, who's gonna look after it?

She'll come round.

Know what? I'll let her name it.

Buy her that Merc – *get this one second-hand* – let her live a bit.

Who wants to live forever?

It's just tears.

She get over it.

(TEL turns back to AKIM, kneeling on the ground.)

What, 's he fucking praying?

*

TEL: Oi, Harry!

(AKIM turns round – from packing his bag.)

What we gonna do about you?

Can't get you in the boot. It's full.

What if you get caught?

AKIM: You want to carry me?

TEL: Leap in the dark, n't it?

Why should I risk it?

(AKIM reaches into his sock and holds out a tooth.)

Stone in yer fucking shoe?

(AKIM hands it to TEL)

AKIM: Gold.

(AKIM shows his gap.)

It's clean.

TEL: … What d'you want, fucking pity?

AKIM: I have two of those.

To pay the way.

You are talking to yourself. You can talk for me.

TEL: You got me wrong, bruv.

(TEL pockets it.)

Keep me going, I'll give you the fare.

I get you to the boat. But then you gotta walk on yer own.
I don't know ya.

(AKIM and TEL look at each other.)

What d'you want me to say?

AKIM: … Nothing.

TEL: Don't think it's just you.

You're here now.

No one loves anyone. Care's gone out the economy. You have to put up with what it shits out of its arse. That's all yer gonna get.

AKIM: That's all?

TEL: That's it.

AKIM: … Thank you for the chance.

TEL: *(Shrugs.)* I see you the other side, now, that's a different matter.

Put yerself in my shoes. I can't risk it.

AKIM: I know you have someone waiting for you. I don't know anyone waiting for me. It doesn't matter.

TEL: … We'll see about that.

Let's see how it goes, eh?

(AKIM nods.)

They let you through, how do I know how to get rid of ya?

AKIM: Wipe your face. I'm gone.

(TEL laughs and flings his arms wide.)

TEL: Yeah, come on, fuck it.

Fuck it.

See if that works when they stop yer.

*

SCENE TWO
GOOD COP, BAD COP

Two plainclothes policemen, TONE and LEE, lolling by an unmarked car, leaning and standing – to one side of a streetlight. They are armed with concealed hand guns. The only thing that identifies them are the police caps they keep close to hand.

TONE returns to the car, zipping up from taking a leak.

LEE: What's that, prostate?

TONE: Ay?

LEE: Keep pissing in that hedge you'll kill it.

TONE: Everyone got their own way to get ready. I want to feel light so I'm up for it, ay?

LEE: Alright, old man.

Back in the car?

(A phone starts ringing, they both look out front to see whose it is. TONE answers his mobile. 'Yah', scribbles down on a notebook, nods 'Great' and pockets the mobile.)

TONE: You get in. Prostate calling…

LEE: Seriously?

TONE: Got to answer the call. When it comes.

LEE: I was you, I'd get that seen to.

(TONE walks round and imposes himself, an arm round LEE's shoulder, pulled tight.)

TONE: But you're not, ay?

(LEE doesn't move; TONE releases and goes back round.)

LEE: … You do know – some people – it's serious?

TONE: Not bothered. When you got to go… you go.

LEE: *(Shrugs.)* Your funeral.

TONE: Still get it up. The force is with me.

LEE: *(Waves it away.)* Too much information.

TONE: It's when it dribbles, know what I mean? Go on
forever, shaking it – getting the last drops out – this way,
that way, up, down, round the houses. Have to stand there
start texting.

LEE: Gross.

TONE: What's yours do?

LEE: *(Gestures at the notebook.)* What they say?

TONE: Go on, then, give a look at your tits.

LEE: … Zip up, your cock's swinging.

TONE: *(Checks.)* Don't be like that.

LEE: You don't respect me.

TONE: Thought you girls were different?

LEE: Too bloody right. We'll cut it off.

TONE: Be worth it though, is it?

See what you got – no one looking.

LEE: None of your business.

TONE: So it's true?

LEE: Nothing to see. Move on.

TONE: Interesting.

LEE: *(Shrugs.)* You've got that out in the air.

What's that change?

TONE: … Nothing.

Your cover's blown.

But you already knew that.

The apple, the jaw – looks really life-like.

Where she gone? She in there somewhere?

Can't be easy, ay? Doing this job.

Not a girly job, is it?

LEE: There's every kind of man.

This is the man I am.

Get over it.

TONE: Blokes or birds?

You even like me?

LEE: What would your mum say if you took me home?

(Pause.)

TONE: She wouldn't like it.

LEE: Case closed.

TONE: Don't know so. Found my stash of *Asian Babes*, didn't say.

LEE: … How d'you know?

TONE: How do I know what?

LEE: How d'you know she found them?

TONE: Stacked up tidy, left them on the kitchen table.

LEE: *You* didn't say anything?

TONE: Like what?

LEE: *Hello mum, what's for supper?*

TONE: … You got a mean streak in you.

LEE: I know mums. And their little boys.

TONE: That's getting personal. Anyway, sticky pages, couldn't get them open.

Shame.

LEE: Don't be a dinosaur, pops, you should go digital.

TONE: Yah.

Newsagent – Mr Patel – *says* they gone out of print. All Muslims. Had to cover up.

It's a new world.

Back to work, ay?

(TONE turns to walk off.)

LEE: What you got?

TONE: … Different car. *(Opens and hands across the notebook.)* They've tracked down he's rented a Merc. *S-Class*. White. That's the reg. Extreme caution.

LEE: Why would he be carrying if he's not on the job?

TONE: He organised the firearms. The grass says he's the connection. If they're tooled up, what's to say he isn't? Safe than sorry.

LEE: *(Hands it back, shakes his head.)* Sideshow.

TONE: That's what you think.

LEE: We've had the briefing, that's what I know.

He's stolen goods, handling – in over his head. Bring him in.

TONE: *(Looks at his watch.)* Should be taking them toe-rags any time now. Be a nice surprise down in Vauxhall. What's the bet there's blood on the pavement?

LEE: Not what you want. Is it?

TONE: Put yourself in the picture. Armed robbery. You're pumped up. All that adrenalin, got to go somewhere. 'Course you put up a fight. Your fault going tooled.

LEE: Wish you were there?

TONE: Pavement ambush… It's a buzz.

LEE: Not tonight.

TONE: *(Looks at his watch again.)* Hear the planes start up, all be over. Time flies.

LEE: What if it's a copper?

TONE: Ay?

LEE: You've bet it's a copper gone down?

TONE: Not the way I've gone in. Not a chance.

LEE: You're not there.

TONE: No, I'm here with you. Anything could happen.

(TONE turns away for a leak, giving LEE a long sideways look.)

LEE: Stand down, Sergeant. It's just surveillance. Loose ends.

(TONE finishes and zips up.)

TONE: It's just mopping up, where's your mop?

Way I see it, you're either a thief-taker, or you're not.
What are you? One of those fast-track degree coppers on
the way up? Too busy to learn the job? Too soft to punch a
villain? Head in a book?

LEE: Psychology, Sergeant. Criminals, and how they think.

(Pause.)

TONE: Do they?

Better call me *Tone*, Sergeant, or we'll get mixed up. Long
night, you might be getting your wires crossed.

LEE: I'm wide awake, Tony.

TONE: *Tone.* Mum's Dutch.

LEE: *Sergeant* Lee Grant. You can call me Sergeant, Tone.

(TONE, a mirthless laugh, moves across to look round the corner.)

Don't get seen. The other unit's got eyes on.

TONE: You get in and lean back, love. I'm on the job.

(Looking out.) It's just poking about out there, why we authorised?

(Pause.)

LEE: Everyone is. No surprises. Precautionary.

TONE: *(Shrugs.)* If this one's driving about, he could turn up.

Got to know what he thinks, what he's gonna do.

LEE: *(Shakes his head.)* You see him?

No fixed abode. Could be parked up somewhere. This is just
one of the places he goes.

TONE: You're not getting it. That's police bollocks. This is his
squeeze – where's he put her? *Shooter's Hill.*

LEE: … So what's that, big man, a joke?

TONE: *(A sorry shake of his head.)* It's that road there.

Work it out.

He's a show off – *and* a coward – won't go on the job himself. So what's he up to? 'Course he's got a hard on, he's about to pull it off. This is where he's coming, all over her. Job done. You're up for some action tonight, girl.

(Pause.)

LEE: You should lighten up.

TONE: You should get ready.

There's a bad man coming.

(TONE takes out and checks the magazine of his Glock hand gun, replaces it in his belt.)

LEE: That's not the way this is going.

(TONE smiles.)

What makes you so sure?

TONE: I forget, you been flown in. Play it by the book, ay?

LEE: Just doing my job.

TONE: We all say that. Don't help us, does it?

(Pause.)

LEE: It's your patch. Play it your way. I'm along for the ride.

TONE: That's better.

LEE: … What's this – Terry what's his face? What you got on him?

TONE: Dirt.

Terry *Dolan. Tel* to his mates. Not that he's got any. *Don't tell Tel, he'll tell everybody.*

LEE: … You know him?

TONE: I know where he drinks. I'm in there.

Watching.

It's *him* they don't want. Not in their clubhouse. They're well behaved – regular, hard-working – thieves – keep it calm. No drugs, no shooters.

He's a liability.

Big mouth. Hoovers it up. Screw loose. Dirty round the edges, know what I mean?

Dirty glass.

No one touch him. Can't work with that. Give the game away.

Just leaks out.

Watch him kick off, smack his woman about – piss you off.

Wouldn't it?

Like that's how you do it. Shut her the rough up. He's in his manor.

(Shakes his head.) Not for long.

Why he's ended up supplying these toe-rags. Smash it up robbers.

He's got into guns.

Cunt's out of control. He's got to go down.

LEE: … That's not your job.

You're working for the police.

49

(Pause.)

TONE: Telling me what my job is – what's so special about you they got you doing the dirty on me?

LEE: I go where I'm sent.

TONE: Not the full back up under fire, is it?

LEE: Why not just keep it quiet?

TONE: Gunman on the loose?

LEE: That's if he turns up.

And he's got a gun.

TONE: So what you worried about?

Nothing to see.

LEE: … You've got form.

TONE: Man down. It goes fast.

LEE: Why's that?

TONE: Hard stop, it just does.

You or them.

LEE: Boy wasn't armed.

TONE: … No, *he* wasn't.

LEE: So what happened? He made a move? You shot the little lookout, got roped in.

The family want to make sense of it. What's gone on?

We all do.

What was he – 19?

TONE: Too stupid to get out the way.

50

LEE: Couldn't see it coming?

    Black kid.

    (Pause.)

TONE: It's stressful what they put you through.

    The mangle.

    You know the mangle they keep for coppers. Ugly old bit of iron.

    They get the handle, and they turn it… and they turn it…

    I came out clean. Back on the job.

LEE: You could have transferred. Ask to temporarily stand down.

TONE: So could you.

LEE: I haven't killed anyone.

TONE: You have to do what you do.

LEE: You crossed a line.

    (Pause.)

TONE: You haven't?

    Come back someone new?

    How's it feel?

    (Pause.)

LEE: … I've had people come at me with glass. Like I'm a faggot, they can burn me.

    I haven't changed. It's always been me.

    But *you*… got problems.

All you *blokes* got problems. Come off you like bullets.

You're not leaving your problems in my body.

TONE: … Starting to get the feel of you.

Let's see, ay?

See if he comes – see how you feel then.

Starts flying – duck.

It's in the training. Do it quick.

LEE: No one's getting slapped tonight.

You can't afford it.

TONE: *I'm* the suspect? What, they think I'll go in too hard?

You think this is me being too aggressive? *(Shakes his head.)*
Aggrieved they put *you* – not just eyes on me – *you* on my
arse.

LEE: Put in a complaint.

TONE: After they accuse me of *what*?

LEE: You tell me.

TONE: … Those cunts.

LEE: You done?

Back in the car?

TONE: *(Scans the inside of the car, distrustful.)* What *is* your job?
Catch me out?

Or wind me up?

LEE: … Why would that be?

People like me, we're the public.

How to keep it safe. You're armed.

TONE: Accredited, authorised.

LEE: Armed.

Stick to the training.

Wait.

Go on waiting.

Take mitigating action. Which I'm doing.

Investigate, assess.

Contain the area.

Communicate with subject –

TONE: Decisive action. – The critical shot.

(Pause.)

LEE: You're on your own.

What you gonna do?

TONE: Take you with me?

(Pause.)

LEE: … Not tonight.

My advice… Sit in the car – wait, let them get eyes on. Hang back, no one gets hurt.

It's over. He goes to jail. You get a clean slate.

I go away. It all goes away.

(TONE grins.)

TONE: … First time, ay?

Don't be scared.

LEE: … I'm giving you options.

You won't be pissing on the side-line – no one there – you get back in.

Clean bill. They let you wipe it. Back on the pavement – no question marks.

No one in your way.

TONE: *(Walks back over to the corner and looks.)* I'm just out for a stroll, walking up the road – *you're* looking round the corner.

LEE: Seeing what you want?

TONE: *(Looking back round at LEE.)* And taking it.

(Pause.)

LEE: *(Shrugs.)* He don't turn up, there won't be anything to report.

TONE: *(Grinning.)* Don't make me laugh, ay?

I know how it works.

What you say and what you do won't meet in the middle.

But it doesn't matter –

They sent you. Put *you* on my arse, they want me to know – *Sit on his arse, tell him he's fucked* – ay?

I'm out.

… What's it matter?

Suspect's on his way.

(Pause.)

LEE: You're on a cliff. It's the wrong step.

TONE: No one's indispensable.

(Pause.)

You like football?

LEE: *(Shrugs.)* Watching my brother.

TONE: You got a brother? You see him?

LEE: … I see him.

TONE: Dresses up? What's he like to do?

LEE: … Score.

TONE: Oh, he's a footballer?

LEE: … Yeah.

TONE: Fancy that, ay?

We don't all do it for the money.

You got to love it.

LEE: He can't kick a ball straight anymore, he's on methadone.

TONE: Yah, I know.

(LEE flinches, taken aback.)

You know how leaky it gets in there. Should by now. Pillow talk, whispers – *Check the photocopier.* Empty the bins, ay?

See *you* coming. See it up on the screen when they gone for a leak.

The skills. Don't leave a trace.

There's disagreement. But the buzz – that's on my side.

It's who you know – not the rules – *people* keep it sane.

(TONE steps round, taking possession of LEE, steering him towards the corner.)

So I've had a think… You haven't seen the bigger picture. They haven't told you.

This my shout.

(TONE steps back and points up from the corner.)

This girl up here?

Beverley. Nice girl. Why she ended up with him… He's led her a dog's life.

It's *her*. She's the grass.

(Pause.)

LEE: … Why wasn't that in the briefing?

TONE: *(Shrugs.)* It's intel. Need to know. You didn't hear it from me. Slipped out.

Talked him down the river, telling me what's going on.

Don't get a woman wrong.

Should have kept it in his pants.

LEE: You? Telling you? … That's not what they – Witness protection?

Does he know?

TONE: *(Shrugs.)* Word gets out.

I'm in there, having a drink.

Listening.

She's crying, I give her a shoulder.

She's giving it away.

Has to get these calls – all hours – telling her she's a dry stick. And he's fucking someone else. Some slut down the phone.

Then he's give her a fright. Brought guns.

Bingo!

LEE: … Keep it down. He'll hear.

What else d'you get?

TONE: Don't be heartless.

Her heart's broken.

That's the problem.

Nice girl – *Beverley.* Emotional. They want you to sort their life out.

I got the trust.

I'm good at what I do.

Get her so far – she's talking – they make me hand her over.

She's the source. Has to go to the handler.

'Course she clams up.

Broke her trust.

They've fucked it, she's run for cover.

We gone blind. Don't know *where* he is.

She stopped coming out to see me.

They didn't tell you?

Nice girl – *Bev.*

Black girl.

She's terrified.

He'll find out.

LEE: … You've put her up as bait.

TONE: What's the odds, ay? Narrowed?

LEE: You won't get away with that.

TONE: Not me, I don't allocate the deployments. Wasn't me decided I should get shuffled off sideways for wanting to do my job – *Here, you have the graveyard shift.*

I've took what's come.

… Beautiful girl.

Woman. She got needs.

Said I'd keep her safe.

Don't make promises you won't keep – if you can help it.

That's the thing about the force – don't co-operate, you're on your own.

She got no way out.

He's got a bone to pick with her.

Let's see.

But I don't see him coming quiet, ay?

(Pause.)

You shitting me. They didn't tell you?

Sent you in blind – half-cocked…

Blimey, that's a discrepancy.

Why'd you fall for that?

Maybe they got their wires crossed. Didn't look into it properly.

Something's gone wrong.

Put you in harm's way – *Don't tell him. See if he's bent.*

Think maybe they don't care about you.

Ay?

(Pause.)

Don't let it come to tears. Only blur your edges.

(Pause.)

LEE: *(Shrugs.)* … Changing how I feel.

TONE: Crack on.

We need to be straight on it – the subject vehicle – no deviations.

Or you can't do the job – you haven't got the balls?

(TONE deliberately turns his back on LEE, placing himself on lookout.)

LEE: … *Everybody* knows, but me? *(Slowly nods.)* How's that happen?

(Shrugs.) Walk away, don't look back. What's to stop me? Hand it all in. Warrant card, the lot. They haven't got my back.

Every alarm bell in my body. Here's how I get punished.

(Shakes his head.) I'm not a *bloke*. I walk a straight line every day *just* being me. Someone gonna knock me off. Something gonna catch me out.

I can't duck it – even if I could. It's coming.

TONE: … Had your chance.

(Pause.)

LEE: I'll put that in the report.

… Same chance you give her in there – *Beverley*? What chance d'you give her?

Get caught out.

Have to wait for someone to come and kill me?

(Shakes his head.)

I've had it. I'm tired of it.

I joined because I was tired of it. Stop and search here, grope you there – queer gear – bang you up against a wall.

Manhandled so you *must* be dirt.

I've got the scars.

I'm a police officer. I say what goes.

… You don't get to shoot him.

TONE: *(Shrugs.)* He's in the way –

LEE: He'll go to jail. Firearms – that's a long stretch.

TONE: *(Turns to LEE.)* Don't make promises you won't keep – ay?

LEE: She doesn't need you to kill him.

TONE: How would you know?

(The sound of the first plane overhead has been building to a rush, it rumbles past overhead. TONE looks up.)

… Face it.

You're out of time.

He didn't cooperate.

(Nods to the side.) Dead man, resisting arrest.

(Plane recedes. TONE puts a conciliatory hand on LEE's shoulder.)

I interviewed a bloke once, had a sexual interest in killing.

Had to, in the end.

LEE: *(Looks at TONE's hand.)* … What happened?

TONE: Had to let him go. Bought himself a day. Jumped off a bridge.

It was already too late.

(LEE looks for a way out.)

LEE: … Tired of living with your mum? What's the end game?

TONE: I'll let that pass. Rookie you.

LEE: Retire on the pension? You've got a property portfolio they're looking into. Where's that come from?

TONE: Perks of the job. What have I got to lose?

All the above.

Brief life. Make it count.

Beautiful girl – in distress.

You tell me I done the wrong thing – doing my job.

Now I'm doing the right thing, ay?

He's a villain.

LEE: You're a copper.

(TONE looks around, no one else there – nods.)

… What if he's not armed?

TONE: What if he is?

LEE: You could get killed. He's not worth it.

TONE: Someone could.

LEE: … Why you doing this?

What's she give you?

TONE: That's *not* what I'm saying. Listen to what I'm saying.

LEE: Want him out the way, just bring him –

TONE: You've asked a question, listen to the answer.

LEE: No one needs to –

TONE: Stop gobbing off.

(LEE's struggle subsides.)

… That's better.

Don't get me wrong – it's not about falling for her. That's a perk.

The price you pay.

The price I *don't* accept – They ask you 'do a dirty job. Then – when you're dirty – they don't want to know. They point the finger of suspicion on you.

Integrity?

(Shakes his head.) Rage.

Send you out, cut you loose – kill you off, ay?

Reap the percussions – always knew something terrible come out.

This one's on them.

They have to explain it.

I stopped a dangerous criminal. How am I a danger?

Ay?

See them scramble 'get on board.

(Pause.)

LEE: Why you telling me?

TONE: Telling you what? It's just banter.

LEE: … How do I come out of this?

TONE: Your way out?

That's up to you.

You won't get anywhere squealing on me.

They won't want to know – want it buried.

No one likes a snitch. Who are you to judge? It's not *policemanly* to snitch on your work mates.

Could get hurt.

(Pause.)

LEE: … I'd have to change who I am.

TONE: Doing this job change you. But you got to go all the way. Man up.

You have to like getting dirty.

Not just feeling dirty, ay?

(TONE puts on surgical gloves – pulls out a cloth-covered handgun and empties it into his other hand.)

Insurance.

Broke his promise. She asked me 'get rid of it. *(Folds it back into the cloth.)* Put that in the car.

(Pause.)

LEE: You gonna have to shoot me.

(TONE looks at him, a puzzled frown.)

TONE: *(Softly nods.)* That bad?

(Folds away the gun and the surgical gloves.)

LEE: Puts me where you want me.

Caught in the crossfire?

I can't change who I am.

TONE: Step out the way. Don't be brave about it.

Just have to shoot your gun.

Bit of Glock smoke.

We both did it.

What's that say?

Reached for it… *Officers responded.*

LEE: It's murder.

TONE: That's ugly.

But then, where *is* that girl you used to be?

What you done with her?

Take hold of her body, squeeze the life out of her.

Shocking.

(Shrugs.) It's done now.

You choose: the head or – the heart?

Can't leave her hanging about.

Got to get a grip.

Who do you want to die as?

(Pause.)

LEE: I don't.

TONE: … See? Bloke came out top.

You pass.

(Pause.)

Keep on side – I got your back.

You're a good bloke.

We all need insurance.

(Pause – LEE begins to shake his head.)

LEE: You make the jump on your own.

TONE: … Don't blame me.

You're off the cliff as it stands. You're coming.

(LEE shakes his head.)

LEE: You take the plunge. Not with my life.

TONE: What life?

Live a little bit.

(… LEE reaches to his pocket, and stops as TONE stiffens.)

LEE: You got that wrong.

I'm not your way out.

(LEE slowly continues into his pocket and takes out a packet of cigarettes.)

Can't stop you – I wouldn't have a leg to stand on.

You can't shoot me unless he comes.

I got time.

(LEE takes one and offers TONE, who shakes his head. LEE lights up and puts the packet back in the pocket.

The second plane passes over.)

TONE: Think about it. *(Looks at his watch.)* Get that call any minute.

Choose life.

(The plane recedes.

LEE takes his time – drops and stamps it out.)

LEE: I believe you. You tell me he's a bad man. – He can't change?

… What tells me to stop you walking off the cliff?

You want *me* to catch you?

Can't save everyone.

Save me.

TONE: How's that?

LEE: … Still got a grip, on who *I* am.

She's not dead.

Just she turned into me.

Get away from people like you – telling me who to be, what to do.

Like you own me, in a dirty mag.

(Shrugs.) From I got no say…

Girl been too *black*, too *butch*, too long.

Don't have to go down feeling guilty. Stand there on the edge like it's my fault, I got it wrong – I took somebody's life and they won't forgive me – what I want's as ugly as me.

Wanting to end it.

I got a life.

That's what *my* mum says.

She got me back.

Good Christian woman – *You have to break the power of death.*

Walk across that bridge – see it the other side.

Don't have to be good, be nice about it – that person's gone.

I don't have to do anything.

Just watch. Let you work it out.

Got my own skin to save.

TONE: She's gone, why she talking to me?

(LEE recoils – a flicker of recognition – smiles and shrugs.)

LEE: … My bad.

Just when you think… You think you've put her away.

Someone like you wants a look.

… Must be *you're* on the way out.

That prostate's ready to kick you to dust.

Look on the bright side.

Stop waving the gun about, you can live without it.

No-body's perfect.

Not in my book.

TONE: End up like you?

Queer copper – shooting blanks?

Wrong body? Trying to get out?

Still got to make it happen.

LEE: … But you don't know what that is, do you?

It's out of your reach.

All that *male privilege* – don't see it – take it for granted.

(Places the muzzle of two fingers on TONE's chest.)

You have to get used to it, people giving you space. Respect.

It's not all backslapping.

Some blokes – so soft, so subtle, so under the radar –
didn't occur to me, till after. What just happened.

I'm a *bloke*, now…

But I know stealth when I see it.

That's not you, is it? Doing your job?

Get in there, undercover?

Corner the girl – black girl – hold her down.

Control her, let her feel the pressure.

Don't love her – just you playing a role.

Good cop, bad cop.

But it don't feel right. Playing with other people's lives.

Where's yours?

You've had enough. You want to be caught.

TONE: That's what *you* say.

I don't need you to tell me what I want, ay?

LEE: What *do* you want, Tone?

Take a girl to the edge? Give a push?

How's it feel?

Never enough?

TONE: … All that? Psychology?

Everyone guilty somewhere. If you look.

Search me all you want. *Got to have cause.* You won't find a wrong-un.

Got to be able to grab it. You got nothing on me.

I'm not the problem, you are.

LEE: … Let's see what hits the ground.

(A personal radio unit sounds; both look to see whose it is.)

On you go.

No one stopping you.

(TONE answers it, 'Yah'. He starts to nod slowly, 'Yeah', and hangs up.)

It's him?

TONE: … No, car crash.

He's dead.

At the scene.

(Pause.)

LEE: … So.

What's the agreed form of words?

Officer requests to step down.

Make up a reason?

TONE: … He's already dead. Who cares? You deal with it.

Any way you turn it, I come out clean.

Did my job.

LEE: Unauthorised firearm.

TONE: … Keep telling stories. Watch how far you get.

Know when to back off. Lick your wounds.

I'm going for a slash.

(TONE wanders off for a leak.)

LEE: … Man down.

(Sound of the next plane coming overhead.)

*

SCENE THREE
GIRL ON THE EDGE OF A BRIDGE

AKIM in his barely legal taxi. Where have we seen him before? Dressed now in different second hand clothes. He stands waiting for his fare to come, looking up directions on his mobile.

BEV arrives and stands in behind him.

BEV: 'Evening.

… Hello, driver?

AKIM: Yes, going where?

BEV: The Elephant, please.

(AKIM glances up at the mirror, and down at the phone app.)

AKIM: That's near…?

BEV: The Elephant & Castle. Down the Old Kent Road.

(He looks up again at the mirror.)

AKIM: You can direct me?

BEV: *(Looks at him, shifts forward to point out the* way.*)* Down here to New Cross, the bus garage – right down the Old Kent Road, all the way – follow it left at the flyover, down there.

Going bowling.

(Shifts back.) Put your global thingummy on? She talk to you.

AKIM: Ah, for now it's just – *(Holds up his barely smart mobile.)*

BEV: *(Nods.)* … Just as well – she only speak to you – that creepy voice.

(AKIM drives off, looking in his mirrors, but dividing his attention with looking up on the app.)

I tell you as we go?

(AKIM nods humbly and puts away the mobile.)

Go on, through Deptford, round the one way at New Cross, the garage is just up there after the railway bridge – you go right.

AKIM: Thank you.

(Pause.)

BEV: Sorry my voice – I've had a cold.

Time to go out.

AKIM: *(Looks in the mirror.)* It's 24 hour?

BEV: … The bowling? Don't know. Should have looked it up.

AKIM: It's late, now – nothing's open. It's gone 12. Everything is closed.

BEV: Is that the time? Runs away. Never mind, just go on.

AKIM: Which place?

BEV: … Go on the Elephant. Just go straight over the roundabout – they've twisted it 'round – but straight over, then left by – Bedlam – they don't call it that anymore – anyway by the park – the War Museum, with the guns – there's that Peace Garden, Dalai Lama – and straight on. Lambeth bridge. Find my own way from there.

(AKIM glances in his mirror, looks ahead and says nothing.)

… Or, no. Just keep going straight – get you to Vauxhall, the A road. Drop me by the river. I can walk up the embankment from there. It's not far.

Tell your troubles to the river. You do that?

AKIM: … No.

BEV: Let it all go under the bridge.

We do.

Must be why it's so dirty.

AKIM: There's no one there. You won't find –

BEV: It's alright. There's always someone in a cab.

(AKIM nods.)

I'm alright.

Do you mind?

Put the music on if you want.

AKIM: No, it's not working.

(BEV looks, nods.)

BEV: … Old time mini cab – still got that smell. Nothing
work, tied together with string, but it goes.

AKIM: I can't afford –

BEV: Don't worry – it's good enough.

Used to get five of us squeezed in up the West End for a
fiver – girls go in free and it's vodka and orange all night
with the late cabbies ogling you legless. Still get you back.
Who knew the radio don't work and the wheel's coming
off? You just get the bruise the next day from a spring
popping out the seat…

AKIM: *(Shakes his head.)* No – please.

BEV: Sorry, I didn't mean to offend you.

No shame being skint.

It just took me back being a girl. Getting taxis – didn't
matter how you got drove, who wants to live forever?
The excitement, this was it, night out, all the girls…

The boys have to walk and get the bus.

You didn't need 'em.

Then you find the one, fall in love and it ends. Something takes over…

(Pause.)

I can't see it no more.

It just floated away.

(BEV looks around her, a stranger.)

Your cab's very nice.

You got nice eyes – kind. Kind eyes.

Can I talk to you?

AKIM: *(Nods.)* No, please.

BEV: Start again with strangers, don't ya? Don't have to tell your name.

AKIM: … Where now? Straight on?

(… BEV nods.)

BEV: Straight all the way.

(Pause.)

You didn't grow up here, did you?

I did. It's what I know.

Treat you like shit.

Maybe there's somewhere better. I never saw it. You see some beaches, palm-fringed. But that's just a dream for rich people. It's not real.

Deptford's real.

The wet streets and the orange street lights and the cars at night…

(AKIM glances up.)

I mustn't forget to pay you.

AKIM: … You can call me George.

(Pause.)

BEV: Do you have a partner? Someone you live with?

AKIM: … No.

BEV: When you do… be careful what you say, because you can't take it back once you've said it.

I've said some things.

Whatever you do – don't treat her wrong.

Don't betray her. Just don't betray her. Bring down the worst in her life, put that in her body.

Put a man in the ground – it's you next.

Don't do it.

AKIM: Someone's dead?

BEV: … Don't look now.

It's not fair on you driving your cab.

Only put me to shame.

AKIM: *(Shakes his head.)* I don't mind.

BEV: … What day is it?

Feels like yesterday – and it wasn't. But you can't catch up. Your life just stops.

Out of the blue.

Colour drops out the sky. It's just grey – everywhere you look.

Can't sleep, tell him don't snore. He's not listening.

Never fucking listened.

He's not there anymore.

Just you.

Then he turns up – sock under the bed – the smell of him. Like he's still there running 'round, looking – *Whose funeral's this?* – and you can't answer, he can't hear you.

It's yours.

It's yours.

And I want you back.

(BEV collects herself.)

… No one there see him buried. Not even his sister. People stayed away. They think he's a grass.

(AKIM glances up, doesn't get it.)

Talk to the police?

(Shakes her head.)

He wasn't a bad person.

Didn't kill anyone else.

Just happened. Went across three lanes, crashed over the side.

People watched it.

AKIM: … An accident?

BEV: *(Shakes her head.)* ... No reason.

Drove himself off the road. Coming into London – nearly home – slipped off...

(BEV shakes her head.)

And for what?

I told him not to go. *Her or me.*

Glitter pants. What's she got?

... Get himself killed. Bring him back in a box you could fit a baby.

He didn't have to.

He had me.

(AKIM nods.)

AKIM: I see.

(BEV shakes her head in answer, and opens a compact mirror out of her bag – looks at herself.)

BEV: Not the one in the mirror, *me.*

Not the one that looked like me.

(Snaps it closed into the bag.)

I had to fight him.

Look how he's come back.

Empty.

AKIM: Look to the future.

BEV: ... I don't know anything about any future.

I had him.

All his faults.

And the ones I never knew.

Couldn't see he wasn't forever.

(Pause.)

My own fault.

It's not nailed down, nick it – she could, glitter pants. I let him go.

Watched him lie to me, pushed him away.

His crooked face.

Drove him to it.

… What I couldn't give him.

Stopped him living.

(Pause.)

Worse things happen.

People moving around – doing their lives – trying 'a get somewhere better. They get stopped.

You get containers of 'em dead. Fishing boats crowded over. That's not good, is it?

You can't come in – boat's full.

Every day a tower block.

See the fire spreading.

There's babies in there.

Is *that* an accident?

And when they do it on purpose? Kill people on the bridges?

Drive cars into 'em.

… Pop a girl into the river. How godless is that?

(AKIM manoeuvres looking into his side mirrors.)

You just get trapped.

AKIM: … What's trapping you?

(For a long time BEV doesn't respond, distracting herself with going through and not finding things in her bag, until she can change the story.)

BEV: … Living here, I suppose. Letting it crowd in on me.

Getting drowned out the way people treat you. Doesn't matter you're English, you're the same – same person – same school, same street – you're black, have to go through all that.

AKIM: You have to fit in.

BEV: Black skin don't fit.

… Not with the police.

AKIM: *(Shrugs.)* To live an honest life is a struggle.

You can't just suit yourself.

BEV: … You have to be a foreigner to work that one out.

It's what you do to survive.

(Pause.)

AKIM: *(Shrugs.)* We have to survive.

You can't blame yourself.

People drown. People have affairs. People –

BEV: No, they don't. Not in this country.

AKIM: Which country? Dead from the neck down?

People are people.

And you – a good-looking woman. You have to take care and go on.

BEV: Keep that dream alive – get a lottery ticket.

AKIM: I don't dream.

Wake up… Don't look back.

BEV: What you looking forward to?

Getting old?

There won't be no pension.

Live off your kids?

They're drowning in debt.

Don't be old, don't be young, don't be sick, don't be black…

That's where we are.

AKIM: You have to breathe – you can't say, *I don't want this one they are breathing here.* Wherever you are, you have to breathe with them.

We won't drown.

BEV: … No?

(AKIM turns around and looks at BEV)

AKIM: We are there.

(BEV looks around, bewildered.)

BEV: … Why did you bring me back?

(AKIM steps out and opens the way for BEV)

AKIM: You are tired.

Go and sleep.

(BEV looks at AKIM)

BEV: You want to come in?

AKIM: *(Shakes his head.)* No charge.

(BEV shrinks from him.)

I'm not judging you.

(BEV steps out, uncertain of AKIM, and walks a few steps.)

BEV: … You've misunderstood.

It wasn't Tel – he wasn't the grass.

It was me.

It was *me. I* talked.

Told him, *Don't bring guns in my life.*

Don't do that to me.

It was his panic. I see that now. Couldn't live normally.

But I couldn't talk him out of it.

I got scared.

(BEV approaches AKIM, puts a finger on his chest.)

Then a man comes along – says he wants to help.

We want the same thing.

Know the same people.

Said it wouldn't have to come out.

He could make it all stop.

… Couldn't see the trap.

I was on my own.

(BEV shakes her head.)

… Someone to listen.

See? You don't look so innocent to me.

(BEV takes cash out of her bag, presses it into AKIM's hand.)

I pay my way.

You turn up now. That man – turns up at the funeral.

Who expected that?

He's left the police, we're free.

What the fuck's that mean?

… That bastard, he'll put it about it's me.

I'll be dead.

Even if I was white – *Black slag!*

Didn't think I had anything to give him…

You make a mistake you have to go on making it?

That's what it costs.

Betray someone.

(Pause.)

Still want to rescue me? Talk me down off a bridge?

Let him go on using me – is that a life?

(Pause.)

That Tel – Broke every promise. Brought nothing but trouble – Didn't try and control me.

Let me breathe.

Said he loved me.

Who cares? No one cares.

Put a blade of grass round my finger, when he was broke. Said I couldn't lose it – just had to let him keep trying it on.

He *did* – love me.

Would've worked it out.

… Put him in a box.

Too late now.

That's it. Not much change out of that, is there?

Keep it.

Never know how much it might cost – live a lie.

Go on living it.

Stalk you all your life.

Why not move on? Something better?

(BEV turns and walks off.)

TEL: *(Off.)* Oi, Harry!

(AKIM turns to the sound of TEL's voice. TEL enters with a feathered beaver hat in hand.)

You left this in the car.

Put it back on – they're watching on the boat. They can still pull us the other side.

(Placing it on AKIM's head.) Get out the port, then you can breathe.

There you go, *Rasta.*

Too fucking obvious. See him lean over – see you – smell in the car, try and get high.

Just nod – *Yes, offisah.*

AKIM: Thank you.

TEL: Keep the clothes – sorry they smell. Scrub up well, though. *(Shrugs.)* You look the part.

AKIM: *(Nods.)* Thank you.

TEL: Got 'a clothe the poor.

Even if you have to go as me.

AKIM: I don't feel well.

TEL: *(Looks around.)* Stay up on deck – don't chat no shit to no one, just look at 'em. Keep your eye on the edge – sea and the sky – let the moon come up on the white cliffs – keep you steady. Seagull comes, don't try and catch 'em, they'll hover you over the side.

But I know it's rough.

Soon get across.

AKIM: I have to leave you.

(Pause.)

TEL: Yeah – whoever you are.

You're a clean skin.

Don't let me rub off.

(AKIM takes off the hat and gives it back to TEL)

They always stop me.

Wish they would sometimes – stop me getting in trouble.

(TEL pus the hat on his own head.)

Get home find out she's had enough. Don't want it no more.

Just waiting for me to find out.

Who wants to be me?

… Done your bit, kept me awake.

Remember keep an eye out – be all over the papers.

AKIM: I'm going now.

(AKIM takes both hands and wipes his face. When he opens his eyes again, TEL is gone.

He steps back into the car – TONE enters to stand behind him.)

Going where?

TONE: Ay?

AKIM: You are going somewhere?

TONE: *(Nods over his shoulder.)* Where was *she* going?

AKIM: I don't know.

TONE: … Keep driving.

Let's have a chat.

(AKIM checks behind him in his wing mirrors, and looks ahead into the audience.)

End.

WWW.OBERONBOOKS.COM